HOW TO BECOME A

SUPER SPEAKER

HOW TO BECOME A

SUPER SPEAKER

The 7 Principles for Speaking with Confidence and Connecting with Audiences

MICHAEL BARRIS

For everyone
who has ever been intimidated
by the prospect of speaking
in front of a crowd …

You can do it!

ACKNOWLEDGMENTS

Even a little book requires a big contribution from various people, and in that regard I would like to express my appreciation to the following: Ulrike Berzau, Mahnaz Dar, Tim Frank, Amy Krick Frank, Shelby Holliman Carley, and James E. Katz. I would not have been able to get this project across the finish line without the stalwart support of my wife, Bonnie Marvel. I am also grateful to all the colleagues, students, clients, teachers, friends, family, and fellow speakers whose voices continue to teach me every day and enrich my work and life.

CONTENTS

Acknowledgments vii

Overview: Tackling Your Fear of Speaking 1

Why Should You Listen to Me? 7

The Seven Principles for Super Speaking 11

Principle No. 1: Make Delivery the Priority 13

    Reflection Corner: What Kind of Speaker Are You? 19

    Reflection Corner: Why Respect the Audience? 21

Principle No. 2: Put on a Show 27

    Reflection Corner: What Audiences Think 33

Principle No. 3: Display Personality 35

    Reflection Corner: Bringing out Your Personality 41

Principle No. 4: Feel the Fear but Keep Practicing 45

    Reflection Corner: From Fearful to Fabulous 51

Principle No. 5: Give the Audience a Reason to Care 57

    Reflection Corner: Inside the Bored Room 61

Principle No. 6: Reveal What's inside You 63

    Reflection Corner: Moments That Moved You 69

Principle No. 7: Make Things Easy to Follow 71

25 Practical Applications of the Seven Principles 79

Conclusion: Close in on Your Goals! 91

Resources 93

About the Author 97

OVERVIEW:
TACKLING YOUR FEAR OF SPEAKING

I saw a study that said that speaking in front of a crowd is considered the no. 1 fear of the average person. No. 2 was death. Death is no. 2? This means to the average person that if you have to be at a funeral, you would rather be in a casket than doing the eulogy.

~American comedian Jerry Seinfeld

Whater makes so many of us afraid of public speaking?

It's clear from the quote above that speaking anxiety is one unbiased, nonpartisan, equitable affliction. It doesn't discriminate. It doesn't care how many times you've already stood in front of a crowd to speak. It doesn't care if you've never stepped on a speaking stage before. It doesn't care if you have an expansive vocabulary, the gift of gab, or even bona fide, first-hand, extensive knowledge of a subject.

FACING THE FEAR OF LOOKING RIDICULOUS
All it knows, by tapping into your fear of not meeting expectations — your own, your peers', your supervisors', your audience's — is that you won't allow yourself to look ridiculous. All you want to do is flee. And you can't do it quickly enough. At the prospect of speaking, your heart races and your palms sweat. You may even feel like throwing up, because you want to avoid what you perceive as a pit of torment — the dreaded public-speaking situation.

Diabolically, your fear strikes at the very things you need to assert yourself onstage: how you use what's in your heart, mind, and imagination to click with the crowd, and how you use your emotional intelligence — that blend of instinct, experience, and practice — to reach out to spectators and say something that truly engages them, even changes them.

Almost no one — I repeat, no one! — is immune to fear. As much as 80 percent of the public can experience it, along with a sense of dread and a nervous feeling in their stomach, at some point in the process of crafting and delivering a speech; but they bear down and get through it. Another 10 percent are said to be hit by debilitating panic attacks and nausea; and an estimated 10 percent not only feel no fear at the prospect of speaking in front of a crowd, but actually love it.

SPEAKING ANXIETY: A UNIVERSAL CONDITION
That said, I have never actually met anybody in the latter group. In fact, based on my experiences as a coach and working the crowd as an entertainer, my view continues to be that fear can attack any speaker at any time, exacerbated by the unpredictability of the speaking challenge.

Even seasoned speakers have to manage not only the fear of not meeting expectations, but also unexpected developments such as PA equipment breaking down, their speaking time getting cut, and audience members talking during a performance — events that can leave them vulnerable to a sudden attack of fear.[1]

---

[1] Nick Morgan, "Why We Fear Public Speaking and How to Overcome It," *Forbes* (March 30, 2011),

The upshot? Speakers are never really safe from the perceived threat to their comfort and security until they've concluded their remarks, said thank you, and stepped off the stage.

Given how much speaking we do in life, isn't it worthwhile to learn how to overcome this anxiety? Or at least to manage it? To keep it from interfering not just with our pursuit of everyday tasks, but with our greater goals and even the achievement of our most cherished dreams? Of course it is!

SPEAKING THROUGHOUT OUR LIVES AND CAREERS

When we're in school, our teachers expect us to give reports of all kinds: on books we've read; on the results of science experiments we've conducted; on TV programs we've watched; on how we spent our summer vacations.

As we climb the career ladder, we are interviewed by hiring managers who ask us where we see ourselves in five years. We communicate with clients on the telephone or by video. We speak in important meetings. We interview people. We impart knowledge in classrooms. We make pitches. And as technology changes, we are obliged to speak both face-to-face and through online communication systems with coworkers in teams.

Outside of work, we talk with sales agents and loan officers about purchases of cars and houses, with doctors

---

https://www.forbes.com/sites/nickmorgan/2011/03/30/why-we-fear-public-speaking-and-how-to-overcome-it/#7e14bbd460b2. Morgan writes that 80 percent of people feel anxiety before speaking but get through it, 10 percent are debilitated, and 10 percent feel no fear.

about medical problems, and with university admissions staff about schools for our kids or ourselves. If we're feeling bold, we might even start up a conversation at a party or a company social event … with a perfect stranger!

The upshot is that speaking articulately helps us handle life's responsibilities. When we meet those obligations through speaking — a deeply personal method of communication — we feel a sense of accomplishment, which in turn triggers a surge of self-confidence that drives us to achieve what we desire most.

HARNESSING SPEAKING POWER TO ACHIEVE GOALS
In the following pages, you'll learn the seven principles for speaking with power: specifically, seven major requirements for making a great impression on audiences, largely through a deeper understanding of how they think and feel. By applying these audience-based concepts to a range of speaking situations, from conferences and business meetings to social gatherings and one-on-one conversations, you will gain confidence and overcome your fear of speaking in front of crowds.

Some chapters include characters who are not real people but composites based on my personal experiences and real people I have met, interviewed, or observed over the years as a musician, journalist, speaker, university instructor, and speaking coach. Unless noted otherwise, any resemblance to specific individuals living or dead is purely coincidental.

Twenty-five clear, concrete suggestions for applying the seven principles can be found in a separate section near the end of this book. But before we hand you the keys to the kingdom, a bit about me ….

WHY SHOULD YOU LISTEN TO ME?

I'm a born entertainer. When I open the fridge door and the light goes on, I burst into song.
> ~British singer-songwriter Robbie Williams

I'm in the back seat of my dad's Pontiac as we cruise down the open highway on a summer afternoon long ago.

Mom sits next to Dad in the front seat, and my sister sits next to me. I'm banging away on the little ukulele I got for a holiday gift, singing my heart out. "Row, row, row your boat, gently down the stream," I belt out in my hoarse eight-year-old's voice. "Merrily, merrily, merrily, merrily, life is but a dream." My parents and sister all join in. "Row, row, row your boat ...."

EVOLUTION OF AN ENTERTAINER
It was here, in the family car, and in the living rooms of my home and my grandparents', that I began my avocation as a musician and entertainer. Whether I was performing for my parents, aunts, uncles, cousins, or grandparents as a soloist or teaming up with my sister who played violin, I got a big thrill out of playing and singing in front of them and having their attention on my performance and the sounds I coaxed out of my little uke.

Switching to guitar at 10, I played and sang at parents' nights programs at my day camp. By the time I reached high school, I was playing assemblies and student council music nights; when I was in college, the venues were coffeehouses and pubs. Eventually, I would perform for scores of people at festivals, concerts, and clubs in the New York–New Jersey area and in Canada, wrapping myself around the jazz and blues music of the 1920s, '30s, and '40s.

I was always fascinated by the craft of working the crowd and by people who did it well. Playing hundreds of engagements, I learned the secrets of grabbing and keeping the attention of audiences.

I refined my knowledge of this subject further when I became a writer. As a journalist, I used my sense of audience to connect with readers of community newspapers, jazz magazines, financial newswires, and news websites. I also imparted my wisdom in how-to articles on stagecraft and a book, *Performing Acoustic Music*.

SHARING THE SECRETS OF AUDIENCE ENGAGEMENT
Inspired by my love of language and my passion for reaching audiences, I moved into speaking — a pastime that led to my becoming a public speaking instructor. As a Rutgers University part-time lecturer, I taught mixed groups of students, including undergrads getting ready to start out in careers, and veterans of the work world.

My happiest moments were seeing the shy, uncertain speakers of the first day of class blossom into poised, confident speakers by the term's end.

Those classes left me eager to share my discoveries with even more people. I strived to be the best model for my own ideas in the talks I gave at service clubs, in my questions and comments as a moderator at marketing conferences, and in the numerous award-winning speeches I delivered at speaking contests. These ideas now drive what I do as a speaking coach.

I draw on this diverse background as I encourage my clients to take their speaking to a new level; as I exhort them to show me the person behind their words, to motivate me to join their exclusive club, to give me a reason to care about what they are telling me.

I know I've succeeded in my quest when my clients demonstrate that they can captivate distracted listeners — including me — with the power of speech.

AN AUDIENCE-BASED PUBLIC SPEAKING PRIMER
Which brings us to this little book. Many articles, books, and courses make speaking sound as if it were almost entirely about the speaker; as if speaking took place in an empty room.

But of course, that isn't true. Speaking is about one thing: how the speaker connects with the audience. You wouldn't be there in the first place if you didn't have an audience, would you? And it doesn't matter if the audience is one person or 100.

Whether you seek to conduct more engaging business meetings, augment the skill set you bring to a communications job, or become a better leader of your community group or sports team, this truism endures: audiences are the beginning and the end of everything in speaking.

With that, here come the seven principles for speaking; seven principles for being engaging, based on an understanding of the reactions and behavior of audiences; seven principles that can help you speak with power, without allowing your fear of the crowd to ruin your message ....

THE SEVEN PRINCIPLES FOR SUPER SPEAKING

I can think of nothing that an audience won't understand. The only problem is to interest them; once they are interested, they understand anything in the world.
  ~Orson Welles, American writer, actor, and film director

The seven principles I've listed below get to the heart of what makes a speech dynamic and memorable. Whether you're crafting a speech or actually delivering it, you need to be mindful of all these concepts, even though certain types of spoken-word activity lend themselves more to some principles than others.

INTRODUCING THE MAGNIFICENT SEVEN
Your speeches will resonate better with audiences if you diligently apply these concepts; but you will soar even higher by employing what I call the Magnificent Seven while working with a qualified coach, mentor, or teacher.

Again, a section on applying these ideas to real-life speaking situations can be found near the end of the book.

So here are the seven principles for super speaking:

1. Make Delivery the Priority

2. Put on a Show

3. Display Personality

4. Feel the Fear but Keep Practicing

5. Give the Audience a Reason to Care

6. Reveal What's inside You

7. Make Things Easy to Follow

PRINCIPLE NO. 1:
MAKE DELIVERY THE PRIORITY

It is important to begin with a statement in your speech that grabs the attention of the audience. I try to make my opening line 15 words or less.

~American radio preacher Charles R. Swindoll

SUMMARY: Content is important, but nothing in public speaking matters as much as the way you convey your message to the audience.

In 1970, a TV actor named Michael Fox — unrelated to Michael J. Fox, the actor in the 1980s TV situation comedy *Family Ties* and the *Back to the Future* movie trilogy — took part in an unusual experiment. Working with a research team, he pretended to be an expert on a fictitious topic and gave a lecture about it in front of academics and professionals who weren't in on the charade.

TAPPING THE POWER OF DELIVERY

Everything that came out of this pretender's mouth was gibberish and double-talk. But what happened when he began to speak on his topic, "Mathematical Game Theory as Applied to Physician Education"? Was the actor who had been billed as "Myron L. Fox," an authority on "The Application of Mathematics to Human Behavior," outed as a fake?

Actually, he was a hit.

Although everything that he told a roomful of psychiatrists, psychologists, social workers, and educators at a continuing education training conference at the University of South California School of Medicine was sheer nonsense, "Dr." Fox's performance received generally glowing audience evaluations.[2]

How did he do that? Amazingly, he delivered his drivel-filled speech with such spirit, warmth, and humor that he won over the audience, even if little he said made sense; and if you're thinking those positive reviews could have been a fluke, consider this: his ruse fooled not just one, but three separate audiences.

To the chagrin of skeptics, subsequent experiments conducted over the years have confirmed this study's findings. Its implications for public speaking could be summed up by the lyrics of a 1930s song by the Jimmie Lunceford Orchestra:

> T'aint what you do, but the way that you do
> it ... that's what gets results.

In other words, when your goal is to make an enduring impression on your audience, delivery isn't simply an

---

[2] Romeo Vitelli, "The Return of Dr. Fox," *Psychology Today*, May 5, 2014, https://www.psychologytoday.com/us/blog/media-spotlight/201405/the-return-dr-fox. The actor's sole knowledge of game theory came from one *Scientific American* article he had read ahead of the role. The researchers, Donald Naftulin, John Ware, and Frank Donnelly, had coached Fox to present his lecture "with an excessive use of double-talk, neologisms, non sequiturs, and contradicting statements," *Psychology Today* reported.

important thing in speaking; it is the most important thing.

CONTENT IS GREAT, BUT DELIVERY IS KING

Taking this idea further: when you connect with audiences, you can have a greater impact than any speaker who attempts to score big with the crowd simply by relying on content.

As a journalist who has written for some of the best-known names in the media industry and as a former member of the faculty of a major American research university, I would be remiss if I did not stress the importance of creating accurate, solid, and valuable content. But as a speaking coach, I urge you to be aware that if your delivery is weak, your beautifully crafted, well-researched content probably won't reach your audience.

But you didn't need a research study to tell you that, did you? Just think of your favorite college professors. What likely set them apart were their delivery (and their personality; more about that later) and the way they held you in their thrall; they didn't drone on about the text. They didn't make a theorem the face of a course. They drew upon their knowledge and passions to create an emotional — and human — experience.

A DYNAMIC DELIVERY MAKES YOU MEMORABLE

It works the other way, too. When I think of students who made the biggest impression on me years ago during my stint as a Rutgers University instructor for an introductory public speaking course, I remember how they spoke and shared themselves with the class, rather than what they spoke about: how they owned their speaking areas, how they connected with the audience, and how natural they seemed. In short, I remember elements of their delivery, not their content.

Why is delivery so important? Because audiences need help. If you want their attention, they need you, the performer, to pull them into the world of your presentation. But they are fussy as well as needy. They aren't going to listen to you just because you're standing in front of them. They need a reason to buy into your story, to motivate them to join your exclusive club.

THE BOTTOM LINE: EARN THE AUDIENCE'S ATTENTION
No matter how rich your content is, or how much time you put into creating it, never assume that a member of the audience will be able or willing to give you the 100 percent attention you think you deserve. That's partly because much of the time they are battling distracting thoughts, instead of listening.

Ironically, speakers often think the audience is laser-focused on their every word. But spectators may not be thinking about the speaker much at all, at least at the outset. Other things — hunger, issues at work, fatigue, stress — are competing for the audience's attention before the speaker even takes the stage. It's another reason to develop a powerful delivery that can cut through listeners' mental traffic, grab their interest, and hold it until the speaker finishes.

What's a "powerful" delivery? There's no definitive answer. Everybody is different, with different strengths and enthusiasms. Different situations call for different types of deliveries, as well. Showing energy and excitement may be appropriate when an upbeat presence is demanded; but a calmer approach may suit a more solemn setting. As a speaker, you could find yourself in both these situations.

But no matter how you speak, you must imbue your words with an emotional edge to turn them into more than just words. Content is great, but it isn't enough to win over the crowd.

That's why Principle No. 1 for super speaking is, Make Delivery the Priority.

REFLECTION CORNER:
WHAT KIND OF SPEAKER ARE YOU?

How would you describe yourself as a speaker? Are you experienced? A beginner? What are your objectives in using the ideas in this book?

_____

_____

_____

_____

_____

_____

_____

_____

How does speaking in front of a crowd make you feel, physically, mentally, or otherwise?

_____

_____

_____

_____

_____

_____

_____

_____

_____

If you have never done any public speaking, how does thinking about it make you feel? If it scares you, what frightens you most?

_____

_____

_____

_____

_____

_____

_____

_____

REFLECTION CORNER:
WHY RESPECT THE AUDIENCE?

Meet Alice.

She is to give a talk at a public library on landmark movies. Drawing on her deep knowledge of cinematic history as a graduate student of film, she has pulled together clips from classic movies to share with her group. However, Alice has little experience giving talks; she got the nod from the library to do this presentation on the strength of her exuberant proposal.

A CAUTIONARY TALE FOR SPEAKERS

Her husband, an experienced lecturer, cautions her to keep the presentation as light and as entertaining as possible for this audience. Owing to the venue — a public library — and the broad appeal of her topic, she can expect her talk to attract a mixed crowd of high school kids, college students, middle-aged movie fans, and seniors. Her husband emphasizes that while many will be coming to learn something, others will be looking simply for a diversion for a couple of hours — and Alice has to tailor her delivery and her program accordingly.

"You should probably also go to the library ahead of time to make sure there won't be any problems with the equipment when you get there," he adds. "You want things to go smoothly, especially since this is new to you."

But Alice never gets around to checking to make sure everything will be in order for her talk, which relies heavily on showing clips of films. Nor does she spend much time thinking of ways to simplify big ideas that underlie academic film books for a talk to a non-academic crowd. She's confident her intelligence and knowledge of the topic alone will carry the day.

She is about to become an example of the pitfalls of failing to do the work to engage an audience and of taking for granted their willingness to bond with a speaker. After you read the rest of her story, share your responses to it in the spaces provided.

THE HARD LESSON

On presentation day, Alice discovers that the projector — which is connected to a laptop that is plugged into wall outlets in the library meeting room — is more complicated to turn on and operate than she realized. She calls for technical help. As the technician gives her a quick lesson in setting up and running the projector, the people she has left sitting in their seats are getting annoyed.

When she is finally able to get the projector going, 40 minutes have gone by. Some audience members now look exasperated, which unnerves her. The rocky beginning sets the tone for the rest of her session. By the time she has introduced her third clip, Alice has learned that coming up with a motivating activity or questions that will spark interest in each film is more work than she realized; the movie's fame or notoriety by itself is not enough — and she is underprepared.

The body language and facial expressions of her audience tell her they are not engaged. She also has to rethink the steps for turning on the projector each time she changes a film clip. Soon, surrendering to rising panic, she stops trying to connect with her audience and just starts showing film clips.

The comments the patrons make to the librarian afterward are brutal. "The teacher could have done more to try to keep us interested," one complains. "I took a shower, changed my clothes, and drove 10 miles for this?" another asks.

When the librarian relays these remarks to Alice, she feels hurt and humiliated. By failing to engage her audience, she let them down. She also let the library down. But most of all, she let herself down.

What's your reaction to this story?

_____

_____

_____

_____

_____

_____

_____

_____

_____

How could Alice have avoided having her talk turn into a debacle?

_____

_____

_____

_____

_____

_____

_____

_____

What was Alice's biggest mistake?

_____

_____

_____

_____

_____

_____

_____

_____

_____

PRINCIPLE NO. 2:
PUT ON A SHOW

I've always known, before I had a record deal, that the thing is to go out and put on the show.

     ~American rapper, singer, and songwriter Flo Rida

SUMMARY: No matter what type of presentation you're delivering, you're putting on a "show" and need to play to your viewers, with an eye and ear to their emotional state.

O n the street corner of a popular neighborhood in a major city, Marty, a guitarist and singer, strives to win the attention — and donations — of passers-by. Busking is not his main gig; his goal is to become a professional guitarist, an ambition he supports by studying with a private teacher, practicing his instrument five hours a day, and accepting legitimate engagements when he can get them. But taking his music to the streets is a way to augment his income while learning how to win over audiences quickly — the mark of a good entertainer, he believes.

TAKING ONE'S CUE FROM STREET PERFORMERS
Marty's heart pounds as he watches the people come and go in front of him on the sidewalk. It seems like a tremendous imposition, his inner voice says, to persuade them to listen to him. But Marty summons the courage to start. He reaches into his repertoire for a flashy tune that showcases his dexterity on the guitar.

Indeed, while most people keep walking, a few stop and turn their heads. One or two draw closer, curious to hear more.

Seeing he has them hooked, Marty shifts gears, launching into a well-known popular song. Belting out this tune with confidence and enthusiasm, he gets the spectators to sing along. Achieving this much so far is impressive: not only did these strangers have no reason to pay him any mind, but they have been hardened over time by endless approaches from peddlers and panhandlers.

THE MAKING OF A SHOW PERSON
But now, pulled in by Marty's infectious energy and showmanship, they can't help becoming absorbed in his performance. "Hey, you are the best back-up singers a guy could ask for!" he banters with them. "When do we go out on tour together?" They enjoy him, but after a few minutes, they need to move on. Marty is gratified to see them reach into their pockets and handbags to pull out coins and bills, which they drop into his open guitar case. "Thanks!" he calls to them. As they depart, they wave goodbye.

Now Marty has to do it all over again. As another group of walkers approaches his space, he shouts, "Hey, everybody, let's celebrate the classic years of rock with a great old song!" and launches into another crowd-pleaser.

And so it goes ....

Marty — and buskers like him, be they musicians, magicians, jugglers, acrobats, puppeteers, or street theater performers — are what you might call pure show people. They need to know how to work the crowd and put on a show that not only captures the audience's attention immediately but — more important — also convinces them to part with their cash.

Speakers of all levels would do well to study the buskers' example. Just like the busker, the speaker — even one addressing a group with a strong built-in interest in the topic — has limited time to engage the crowd. The speaker needs to know how to entice the audience to ensure his words will have impact.

STRIVE TO APPEAL TO THE AUDIENCE'S SENSES
The speaker must arrange the elements of his talk or presentation to get the audience emotionally involved. He is free to use whatever tools he likes, as long as they fit the purpose of the speech, including relying on wordplay or physical motions and changing the sound of his voice.

Depending on the situation and purpose, you, the speaker, can inject some degree of emotional "show," if not out-and-out entertainment, into any type of speech you can think of:

- A spiel to a group of investors
- An overview of an earnings report to investors, analysts, and journalists
- An inspirational speech on bouncing back from setbacks
- A plea for funds for a cause
- An educational talk on an issue
- A debate speech

- A eulogy

Don't let the subject matter — especially that last one — scare you. As a speaker, you should always seek to transport spectators into your world. In serious situations such as a funeral or a financial meeting, using your speaking ability to create an appropriate mood — or to reinforce an existing one — is acceptable and expected.

But don't be afraid to push the audience a bit; add life to the proceedings by wielding your skills as circumstances warrant. One way to do that is by focusing on a pertinent narrative. For instance, at a memorial service, tell the little-known story of how the deceased came to the country with no money, took menial jobs, and eventually turned himself into a captain of industry.

THE BOTTOM LINE: AUDIENCES EXPECT A SHOW
In an earnings conference, play up the underreported tale of the corporate turnaround that began with the company hemorrhaging money in the first quarter of Year 1 and climaxed with its turning a profit by the fourth quarter of Year 2.

Those are ways of working the audience's emotions, also known as "pushing its buttons."

At this juncture, some of you may be grumbling, "Why do I have to put on a show? Isn't it enough that I make myself vulnerable for people by putting myself on display and talking to them? Do I have to entertain them, too?" And the answer is, "Yes. You do."

As soon as you step into a speaking area, you become a performer. The speaking area is a stage — regardless of its size or location. It could be an area in a boardroom, a backyard deck, the bimah in a synagogue, an outdoor stairway, or the expanse of a classical proscenium arch stage. The people gathered around that stage are an audience; and audiences expect performers to put on a show. It's just how we're wired.

If the idea of being a show person intimidates you, here are a few ways you can use the tried-and-true tools of audience engagement to help your cause:

- Talk to the members of the audience as if they were expecting to be entertained, not merely fed a plateful of facts or statistics.
- Vary your vocal tone, volume, and speed to whip up enthusiasm; use different facial expressions and hand gestures to underscore key points.
- Move purposefully around your speaking area to emphasize ideas.
- Listen closely to your inner voice. Be so tuned into the audience's mood that you can feel at a given moment what sort of energy or outreach would work best to engage the crowd.

By making your presentation more like a performance, you will make a strong impact on your audience. Therefore, do as Principle No. 2 says, and Put on a Show.

REFLECTION CORNER:
WHAT AUDIENCES THINK

Imagine you are about to deliver a speech at a public library on a topic you know well. The air conditioning unit is malfunctioning, gradually raising the room temperature. How would these conditions affect the decisions you make about how you deliver this talk? Write your answers below. (Dealing with this particular speaking challenge gets fuller treatment in the question-and-answer section at the end of the book.)

PRINCIPLE NO. 3:
DISPLAY PERSONALITY

Personality is the glitter that sends your little gleam across the footlights and the orchestra pit into that big black space where the audience is.

~American actress, comedian, and sex symbol Mae West

SUMMARY: While a speaker has many tools with which to enthrall listeners, letting audiences see his personality may be the most compelling.

All day at a marketing conference at a midtown Manhattan hotel, executives from across the US have been holding forth on the changes in the business landscape. They are here to enlighten an audience of merchants, marketers, CEOs, and other professionals on the fine points of exploiting customers' addiction to using their mobile phones for everything from diagnosing car trouble to ordering pizza. The goal is to help attendees formulate a business strategy for the months and years to come.

TAPPING THE APPEAL OF IMPERFECTION

Accustomed to speaking publicly, these senior leaders ooze polish and professionalism. They control their narratives well, occasionally using wit to lighten the moment and engage the audience, presenting information that will be helpful in setting medium-term business plans.

Then Arthur takes the stage.

With a broad smile lifting the corners of his baby face, this middle-aged chief marketing officer seems perpetually amused. "Good morning, Eddie, and to Gail and Tony," he calls out to the master of ceremonies who introduced him and to the conference's organizers watching from the side of the ballroom. "And everybody. How are you all today?"

"Good," someone calls out.

"I have an idea what I'm going to talk about, but you know what? It doesn't bother me one bit if I go off topic," Arthur says, impishly. "I think it's more important that we live in the moment. And more fun. Don't you?"

LEVERAGING THE CHARM OF THE QUIRK
A few people clap, uncertainly. Is this guy for real? they wonder. Speakers don't usually exhibit this kind of eccentricity at these forums. Now Arthur throws out a question: "How do you ensure longevity as a business in the mobile communication era?" he asks. As he says these words, he lifts his brows and glances around the room.

"You already know that the world is changing faster and has become more complex than ever, right? So how do we roll with the changing tide? How do we deal with the arrival of very quick, immense, and often overwhelming change that has roiled so much of industry in the last few years?" he asks. The audience is fixated on him now, curious to hear more from this unorthodox speaker who appears to speak from his gut.

"This is a good era to be a marketer," Arthur says. "The appetite for big ideas is big enough for the size of the opportunities — and challenges — we face. And the amount of disruption and excitement — and frustration and liberation — I have seen as businesses in general try to get a handle on the mobile revolution is plenty big."

There is something warm and reassuring in Arthur's idiosyncratic manner. Listening to him feels like having a chat with a neighbor over the backyard fence.

Arthur occasionally fumbles his pronunciation of a word, or struggles to get certain words out of his mouth. But these little stumbles feel like a big part of him. Rather than slow down, he doggedly pursues his point.

THE MOST VALUABLE TOOL IN THE SPEAKER'S KIT
"Some folks are a bit overwhelmed by the mobile revolution. Especially those of us who started well before the internet era," he says. "I'm in the same boat, but I've kept up. That must be why they have me here today." He waits for a laugh. Getting it, he continues: "So, let me give you the newsflash: mobile is here to stay. What's more, it will become an even bigger part of our lives and work as time goes by."

Arthur lets that knowledge sink in as if it were the most important thing he will ever say. Then he says: "This may be hard for you to hear, but in 10 years' time, or less, unless you have upgraded and replaced parts of your operations to thrive in an era of mobile communication, your company will be as obsolete as — what? Give me an example of something obsolete," he says, appealing to the crowd. "Public pay phones? Getting film developed?

Reading newspapers on the train into work? How about Velcro shoes?" The crowd laughs despite its uneasiness at this pessimistic business outlook. "I'm not ashamed to admit that I still have mine," he says. "What it means is, if you don't get with mobile soon, your era will be over."

PERSONALITY IS EVERYTHING THAT DEFINES YOU

Arthur may not exude the same glib coolness as his predecessors; but his blend of direct talk, awkwardness, and life experience is working its magic on the audience. He is connecting with them in a way the smoother speakers before him did not; and he will be remembered for it. Why? Because he is showing an abundance of a quality that is gold for a speaker: personality.

Personality may be the most valuable tool a speaker can employ. Personality is the sum of who you are. It's everything that defines you: your sense of humor, your values, your biases, your fallibility, your quirks.

Effective speakers draw from this bag of traits. It's fascinating to witness, and a crucial part of appealing to the listener's senses and emotions.

Arthur's impact on his listeners is also noteworthy because he was one of the day's last speakers. The attendees, who had been taking in a stream of spoken communication since 9 a.m., were probably suffering from speech fatigue by the time Arthur took the stage, around 5 p.m. But he still managed to mesmerize them, simply by appearing human onstage — and possibly more so than anybody else.

Getting in touch with your personality onstage can be liberating. A comfortable speaker can let himself naturally stumble over a syllable every now and then without panicking. He can spend several seconds weighing what he will say next.

When things are working at an optimum level, an audience sees all these quirks and apparent imperfections as part of the speaker's persona. While this revelation of warts, figuratively speaking, may seem shocking at first, it will also make the speaker stand out. Ultimately listeners will accept it as a tool in the kit of a presenter with a well-heard message. The crowd may not always agree with what they see and hear, but they will remember it.

THE BOTTOM LINE: PERSONALITY IS POWERFUL

When I taught public speaking at Rutgers University, I did an exercise early each semester to highlight the inner power a speaker could unlock by releasing his personality to the crowd. The results were obvious to all; I describe the exercise at the end of this section.

To sum up, nothing is more rewarding for a performer than bonding with an audience. And nothing is more powerful for an audience than connecting with a performer. Letting your personality show when you speak gives your words and actions a profound effect that will resonate with the audience long after you finish.

Consequently, do as Principle No. 3 says: Display Personality.

REFLECTION CORNER:
BRINGING OUT YOUR PERSONALITY

Here is the exercise I did with my Rutgers University public speaking classes to spur the release of personality onstage. Initially, I developed it to discourage students from reading from a phone or sheet of paper a speech they had written out in full sentences. The paper or phone blocked the energy flow between them and the audience.

TRADE FULL SENTENCES FOR KEY WORDS
Converting a written page or "script" into key words and then speaking to the key words allowed speakers to show personality through their word choices, random thoughts, digressions, and even forgetful moments — and to connect strongly with audiences.

Give it a try.

On the lines below, write around 150 words describing your background as a speaker, what you would like to improve about the way you speak, and how much overcoming speaking anxiety figures into your goals.

_____

_____

_____

_____

_____

_____

_____

_____

_____

_____

Now read it out loud, as if you were addressing an audience, using a video feature on your computer or phone to record yourself. Give it the best, most expressive reading you can.

Now watch the video. How does the presence of the paper you are holding affect your ability to reach the audience?

CHOOSE KEY WORDS THAT HELP YOU SHAPE THE NARRATIVE
My hope is that you will notice that the energy goes into the paper into your hand, instead of out to the audience.

Now let's go through what you wrote, line by line.

For each line, choose two to three key words that would help you remember the speech without looking at the paper. The chosen words should set off emotional sparks in you. Note your choices below:

_____

_____

_____

_____

_____

_____

_____

_____

_____

Now, looking only at your key words, deliver the statement again, but this time as a speech, as you gaze in the mirror. Again, record yourself with the video function on your phone. Then view the video.

How was this new version different from the last?

You should see a personality emerging as you spontaneously reconstruct the speech around the key words, using fresh words and ideas that come to mind naturally.

PRINCIPLE NO. 4:
FEEL THE FEAR BUT KEEP PRACTICING

I used to be incredibly afraid of public speaking. I started with five people, then I'd speak to 10 people. I made it up to 75 people, up to 100, and now I can speak to a very large group, and it feels similar to speaking to you one-on-one.
~Canadian self-help author Robin S. Sharma

SUMMARY: Learning to deal with fear is part of growing as a speaker. If you persevere even as panic grips you, you will gain confidence that will both improve your speech and let you gauge the mood of the room and engage in a generous give-and-take with the audience.

I'm not going to lie to you.

Trying to banish fear will get you nowhere. Fear is an innate response to a stressful stimulus. You can no more rid yourself of fear than you can prevent yourself from being startled by a car backfiring or gasping at something jumping out from the darkness in a horror movie. Fear brings about the release of chemicals that increase your heart rate and cause you to breathe more quickly, among other reactions.

WE'RE WIRED TO FEEL FEAR TO AVOID DANGER
These feelings stem from autonomic behavior that is designed to keep us alive. It is as necessary as breathing. So forget about extinguishing your fear of speaking. Ain't gonna happen. But you can learn to function and speak

effectively even as you feel the fear, which is much more realistic than attempting to become truly fearless.

It all comes down to preparation: how much of it you do and how effectively you do it.[3]

Some questions to ask yourself:

- Do you practice your talks sufficiently before you give them?
- Do you create a training system that will make it as easy as possible to learn the speech?
- Do you craft your main points so that you can keep track of them and talk about them naturally?
- Do you effectively use tools such as the video and audio features on your smartphone?
- Do you try to get unbiased, knowledgeable feedback from a coach, mentor, or professor?
- Do you lean too heavily on the opinions of family and friends who may choose to lie rather than hurt your feelings with honest — and valuable — criticism?

Though I'm an experienced speaker, I still need to practice to overcome the acute anxiety I feel before I speak. At some point — generally between getting the speaking engagement and delivering the talk — I'm

---

[3] The fight-or-flight response that characterizes speaking anxiety dates from prehistoric times, when early humans perceived watching eyes as a threat, likely belonging to predators, as noted by Harvard Medical School physiologist Walter Bradford Cannon in 1932.

overcome by dread. I'm generally at ease once I hit the stage. But if I didn't prepare so thoroughly, I wouldn't be.

So how do I prepare?

I record myself multiple times on a third-party video-conferencing application on my computer till I feel the material has sunk in and I can start to concentrate on making it mine. But invariably as I practice, the anxiety grows. I can't beat it, so I've learned to accept it. In fact, I have even come to regard it as necessary, because it pushes me to practice and perform better. You would be well advised to do that, too.

USE PRACTICE TO OVERCOME THE PRE-SPEECH JITTERS
Set aside a block of time for rehearsing and refining your speech. When practicing, make sure you are 100 percent focused on your task. Test the strength of your key words. Do they help you remember the speech as well as they should? Do you need to shorten them or change them? Does the speech take longer than the allotted time to deliver? If so, remove whatever words or pieces you can to get it within the time frame.

Record a video of yourself speaking and play it back. Are you making eye contact with the audience? Are your facial expressions varied? Are your hand gestures and other body motions effective? Isolate what needs work, correct the problem, practice again, and then record it and view it once more.

I strive to reach a point in my preparation where I know my grip on the material is solid. Getting to this state reassures me that I would be able to access the information stored in my brain and deliver the speech without incident, even if my jitters escalated dramatically at any point during the presentation.

That last phrase, "at any point during the presentation," is important, because we never know exactly when anxiety can strike us in the speech-making process. Even professional speakers can experience an unexpected surge of anxiety, no matter how much they prepare.

THE BOTTOM LINE: YOU NEED TO FEEL SPEAKING ANXIETY

But here's the good news: you need to experience some fear to do — and to be — your best. That's because the fight-or-flight response gives us an extra charge of energy and brainpower to react faster to danger.

In fact, many of my fellow speakers agree that if you are too relaxed when you speak, you won't be able to summon the energy you need to put on a truly riveting show. Your lack of anxiety will keep you from unleashing the power surge you need to connect with the audience. Ironically, without fear, you risk failing to engage the crowd. You could end up boring them.

Understand that feeling afraid is part of developing into a stronger speaker. But if you practice despite your anxiety, you'll feel a security that comes with knowing the material.

When you are finally onstage, that self-assurance will let you relax sufficiently to gauge the mood of the room and engage spontaneously with the audience — the essence of putting on a show. And believe me, when you achieve that feeling, it's delicious! It's like getting on top of a big, beautiful rolling wave you've spent weeks finding the nerve to mount with your surfboard, and going on to have the ride of your life.

That joy you feel when you stare down your fear and overcome it is just one of many reasons to make your mantra Principle No. 4: Feel the Fear, but Keep Practicing.

REFLECTION CORNER:
FROM FEARFUL TO FABULOUS

Fear can have two sides — one we associate with self-doubt and powerlessness, and one we experience as a wellspring of energy and drive. The following profile is based on my own speaking experiences and on my work as a speaking coach. As you read it, consider your own memories of and feelings about speaking, and then write about your reactions in the space provided at the end.

A SPEAKER'S JOURNEY

As he listens to his introduction from the wings of the stage, John, a veteran speaker, knows he needs to hook the audience from the get-go. He realizes that at this moment, their minds may be on other things, so he needs to establish quickly that his talk is the only thing they should be focusing on.

Battling fears
Right now, waiting for his cue to go on, John is experiencing his usual pre-speech butterflies. He has that familiar queasy feeling in his stomach; and before the stagehand led him to the wings, he was anxiously pacing in the performers' lounge.

Over the years, John has learned to expect this fear — and to respect it. He knows some fear is necessary to do his best work in front of the crowd. When he is finally introduced and walks onto the stage, he gets a polite round of applause. He smiles as he strides purposefully to the center of the speaking area, pausing to make eye contact with the crowd — and to take a breath. Surveying the faces   before him, he is reminded of the saying:

> Without you, I'm nothing.
> Together, we're everything.

Now, the value of all John's preparation will be put to the test. As he begins, his familiarity with the material calms him. With each passing second, he is letting the crowd get to know him and he is getting to know them.

Reading the feedback

As John moves around the room, he varies his word choices, modulates the tone and volume of his voice, and employs different hand and arm gestures. He makes sure to spend about the same amount of time facing each point of an imaginary triangle he visualizes pointed toward the crowd, so that he can give equal attention to everyone in the audience. Focusing on the spectators' expressions and body language, he uses this feedback to gauge how well he is reaching them.

The smiles and nods John sees reassure him
that he is on his way to winning over the
audience. Now, he loosens up even more. The
ideas he has spent hours refining at home are
flowing out of him, precisely shaped and
organized for easy consumption. His folksy
tone and animated expressions and hand
gestures remind the audience that they're
watching a living, breathing human being; in
short, a personality.

As John relaxes, the spectators, too, are
becoming more at ease with him. They are
forgetting the worries and thoughts running
through their minds. All that matters now is
taking in John's story. The sense that his
musings are heartfelt makes the setting
much more intimate.

Pure energy
A pure energy that makes his brain work
faster and his reflexes sharper kicks in. John
is now where he wants to be — simply
talking to the audience and watching them
stare back, rapt. Speaker and audience have
become one, a coveted but elusive objective.

John has never felt more alive, more
fulfilled, or more the person he was born to
be. It is thrilling beyond anything he has
ever savored. And to think it started with
fear. A fear that — for now — is behind him.

What is your reaction to this portrayal of a speaker? To what degree did it stir up thoughts of your own challenges on the speaking stage?

_____

_____

_____

_____

_____

_____

_____

_____

What does this story tell us about our perceptions of fear related to speaking in front of a crowd?

_____

_____

_____

_____

_____

_____

_____

_____

What caused the speaker and the audience to bond?

_____

_____

_____

_____

_____

_____

_____

_____

_____

PRINCIPLE NO. 5:
GIVE THE AUDIENCE A REASON TO CARE

If you engage people on a vital, important level, they will respond.
        ~British playwright-poet-screenwriter Edward Bond

SUMMARY: Including a few contextual details explaining why your content matters to the audience helps them answer the burning question: Why should I care about this topic?

In October 2001, Steve Jobs, the CEO of Apple, unveiled a device that forever changed the way the world experienced music: the iPod portable music player. Jobs, a visionary, charismatic executive, couldn't have known it at the time, but he was providing speakers with a classic example of how to motivate listeners to care about a speech.

'1,000 SONGS RIGHT IN YOUR POCKET'
In his faded blue jeans and black turtleneck sweater, the legendary entrepreneur held up the original iPod — which he described as "roughly about the size of a package of playing cards" — and said:

> "This amazing little device holds a thousand songs, and it goes right into my pocket."

He continued:

"How many times have you gone on the road with a CD player and said 'Oh, God, I didn't bring the CD I wanted to listen to!' To have your whole music library with you at all times, is a quantum leap in listening to music ... You can take your whole music library with you, right in your pocket. Never before possible."

Jobs's presentation, which can be viewed on YouTube, is studied in university public speaking courses partly for this reason: his constant hammering away at the then-new idea that anyone could have 1,000 songs "right in their shirt pocket."[4]

Including these contextual details accomplished two things: one, it let the audience appreciate the iPod's edge over the then-dominant players in the field, and two, it gave listeners a reason to care about the clever little gadget. And not just to care, but to get excited about it; to exclaim, "You mean I can have all my songs right in my shirt pocket? Wow!"

STRESS THE PERSONAL RELEVANCE OF YOUR IDEAS
Jobs's spiel illustrates that demonstrating the relevance of an idea can pull the audience in.

Over and over again, we see speakers leaving out valuable context because they assume the audience already knows what they are talking about. But by

---

[4] The demonstration is viewable on YouTube as "Apple Music Event 2001 — the First Ever iPod Introduction."

neglecting to put things into perspective, speakers fail to hold the audience's interest.

Why do we need to unearth information that would reveal broader, more fascinating aspects of the subject? Because some people in the crowd may not know just how significant this matter is.

THE BOTTOM LINE: STRIVE TO EDUCATE EVERYONE

There are always people in audiences and in life who don't know quite as much as they think they do. The speaker needs to make sure those people will understand the lecture, too. And even if some folks in the audience are somewhat familiar with the topic, it doesn't hurt to highlight or reaffirm for their benefit why certain information matters. Doing so could even help them connect more strongly with the speech.

But if you don't include these compelling details, you risk losing the audience — and failing to draw the attention your speech deserves, as mentioned in our section on Principle No. 1, Making Delivery a Priority.

Some examples of speeches that neglect to answer the question "Why should I care?":

- A talk on **stroke prevention** that describes the symptoms, causes, risk factors, treatment, and prevention of strokes, but omits the telling detail that strokes kill about 140,000 Americans each year, or about one every four minutes.
- A speech on **the battle over the US-Canada Keystone oil pipeline system** that notes

environmentalists' opposition to Washington's plan to permit the pipeline's completion, but fails to point out that the US government's underlying promotion of fossil fuels marks a major change of direction in American environmental policy.

- A marketing conference keynote address that mentions US consumers' **growing demand for personalized shopping experiences** and engagement, but doesn't connect this request to the broader mobile revolution that allows people to use their phones to compare prices, get product reviews, and buy from anywhere.

When we show people how information relates to their lives, and give them a reason to care about it, we engage with them and leave them with a vivid impression that lasts well beyond the end of the speech.

For that reason, Principle No. 5 is: Give the Audience a Reason to Care.

REFLECTION CORNER:
INSIDE THE BORED ROOM

Think of speeches, lectures, meetings, or discussions that
have enthralled you. How did the speaker, presenter, or
meeting leader organize the material to make you care?

_____

_____

_____

_____

_____

_____

_____

_____

_____

_____

_____

_____

_____

_____

_____

_____

_____

_____

_____

_____

Now think of speeches, lectures, meetings, or discussions
that have bored you. How did they lose you? How could
they have reorganized or otherwise reworked the
communication to get you to care?

_____

_____

_____

_____

_____

_____

_____

_____

_____

_____

_____

_____

_____

_____

_____

PRINCIPLE NO. 6:
REVEAL WHAT'S INSIDE YOU

*You've got to express yourself in life, and it's better out than in.
What you reveal, you heal.*
  ~Chris Martin, lead singer of British rock band Coldplay

SUMMARY: Audiences will connect with you and remember you if you let them catch you in the act of expressing emotion.

We're at a public speaking training class in the New York metropolitan area. The speech portion of our gathering is underway, with several speeches slated to be delivered tonight on various topics.

Speaker no. 3, Marge, has long struggled with delivery issues mainly related to a lack of assertiveness onstage. Tonight, however, she is about to teach the rest of us how revealing intense feelings can electrify the crowd.

LET THE AUDIENCE JOIN YOU IN EMOTIONAL MOMENTS
Marge is delivering a speech on her close relationship with a disabled friend. A few minutes into her remarks, she utters the following words to the 15 people seated in front of her in the office area that serves as our meeting space:

> "She's my closest friend and we do
> everything together — everything her
> limitation will allow. But sometimes, people

avoid her because being around her makes them uncomfortable. And I feel bad for her."

Marge hesitates. As she speaks her next words, her voice breaks.

"And it upsets me so much, because it's not fair," she says.

Suddenly, Marge is crying. "I'm sorry," she says, although there is no need to apologize. "I can't stop thinking about how unkind the world can be." Through her tears, she says: "My friend is the nicest person you will ever meet."

For a second or two, Marge is in sorrow. The audience quietly watches her. Then she pulls herself together. She pushes on with her story and successfully brings it to an end, even completing it within her allotted time.

DRAW IN THE CROWD WITH FEELINGS
The unabashed display of emotion changes the tenor of the room. It pulls the audience toward her.

At night's end, when the votes for the Supreme Speaker award are privately cast by club members and counted, it comes as little surprise that Marge is the winner. She gets to take home a gold sticker with the words "Supreme Speaker" on it and put it in her club achievement record book.

What's the lesson? If you want to be memorable, if you want to make an impact, let your emotions transform you.

You can make an indelible impression on the audience by revealing yourself.

When Marge tapped into her emotions, she triggered a rush of empathy in the audience. If you want your speech to have impact, choose a topic that arouses deep feelings in you — so deep, you can't help revealing them to the crowd.

Producers of television and radio soap operas have long understood the power of tearjerker stories to engage audiences. Yet speakers only infrequently seem to draw from their emotional wellspring. It's not hard to understand why.

- Not all speeches lend themselves well to this action.
- It is difficult to accomplish without the right stimulus.
- Not everyone is willing to make themselves so publicly vulnerable.

But whenever a speaker does express joy, anguish, or any other emotion, count on the spectators to move to the speaker's side, as if by instinct.

TURN PAIN AND JOY INTO MESMERIZING SPEECHES

I learned first-hand the importance of emotion. I was in a regional speaking contest, talking about my experience singing to my ailing mother in the last days of her life while she lay in a morphine-induced coma.

I had chosen to serenade Mom in her private room at the facility where she was living, because in the years prior to her debilitating stroke, she had enjoyed singing. Possessed of an uncanny ear for singing harmony, she had been in an amateur choir, and sometimes when we watched TV as a family, she would spontaneously join the movie or TV show actor singing, in perfect harmony.

My fondest memory of her, I told my audience, was the time the two of us sang a duet, over the kitchen sink, as we did dishes together. Mom washed and sang the harmony while I dried and sang the melody.

"Not only did our dishes sparkle," I told my contest audience, "but so did the harmonies we created as a mother-and-son vocal duo."

ALLOW THEM TO FEEL THE EMOTIONS STIRRING IN YOU
Now, at Mom's bedside, I told the crowd, I decided to sing love ballads from the 1930s and '40s, not only because they were in vogue when Mom was growing up, but also because they were the soundtrack of my parents' courting days. Dad had died the year before, and Mom had lamented on previous visits how much she missed him. So I thought hearing these songs might bring Mom back momentarily. From here, the story gets a bit surreal:

> My mother lay motionless in bed with her eyes closed as I sang Cole Porter's epic love song "Night and Day." As I finished singing the first verse and was about to start the next line, which begins with the words "night and day," something extraordinary

happened. Mom opened her mouth and started trying to sing along with me. The caregiver and I looked at each other across the room; we could not believe what we were seeing.

I felt my audience grow still as I recounted pulling my chair closer to my mother, my feelings beginning to roil. Speaking directly to the figure in bed, I said: "Mom, you love these old songs, don't you?" And Mom, still lying motionless with her eyes closed, opened her mouth and said one word: "Yes."

And those were the last words I ever had with her. Reliving my mother's demise and reexperiencing that one final incredible moment of bonding with her brought me to tears. It took me a moment to regain control of myself before I could carry on, but I did.

Needless to say, the speech had tremendous impact and — just as Marge had done when she spoke about her disabled friend at her speaking training meeting — I won the contest.

If publicly reliving pain — or joy —unnerves you, remember this: exposing your despair or delight to an audience is part of being that "show person" you must become to give your words impact.

If you want to make a big impression on the crowd, pick a topic that resonates deeply with you. You don't have to have a tearful outburst like Marge's, if it's not in you; you just have to be authentic. No matter what you feel, expressing genuine emotions will give your speech undeniable power; and it will be remembered long after you conclude it.

And that's why Principle No. 6 is: Reveal What's inside You.

REFLECTION CORNER:
MOMENTS THAT MOVED YOU

Think of a speech or presentation you have witnessed that elicited very strong emotional reactions from you. What specifically did the speaker say or do that made you feel as you did?

_____

_____

_____

_____

_____

_____

_____

To what extent did he draw out emotions through humor? How would you describe the type of humor he used?

_____

_____

_____

_____

_____

_____

_____

_____

_____

How did he move you with his word choices? What expressions or turns of phrase got the greatest reaction from you?

_____

_____

_____

_____

_____

_____

_____

_____

PRINCIPLE NO. 7:
MAKE THINGS EASY TO FOLLOW

There is a beauty and clarity that comes from simplicity that we sometimes do not appreciate in our thirst for intricate solutions.
~German religious leader Dieter F. Uchtdorf

SUMMARY: Make it simple for audiences to follow your narrative, since they can't play back something you said.

Anthony, a journalist and musician, teaches "Heroes of Pop," an enormously popular non-credit community college course. On the evaluation forms that students fill out at the end of the program, Anthony consistently gets rave reviews for his content, his knowledge, his enthusiasm, and, most of all, his clarity.

Typically, a student evaluation might go like this: "The teacher is always well prepared and keeps things simple and easy to follow." Or: "I never knew there was so much about this topic that I didn't know, and the instructor made his lessons a pleasure with clear explanations."

REMEMBER: AUDIENCES CAN'T REWIND A LIVE SPEECH
Aware that a smooth narrative is essential, Anthony pulls together all the videos, digital recordings, and other materials he intends to use for a lesson, before writing out his lecture in complete sentences.

The narrative is packed with his insights on the personality traits, historic events, and cultural trends that have shaped the careers of the major popular singers of the last 100 years. Its purpose is to set up the playing of an instructive video or recording and the teacher's questions afterward. Then Anthony reduces his long-form narrative to concise key words and statements that become talking points for his presentation.

He keeps his notes on a lecture stand to make it easy to glance down quickly without breaking eye contact with the audience.

SMART OR SILLY, A CLEAR NARRATIVE GETS ATTENTION

Anthony's obsession with making his content easy to follow stands him in good stead. The administrator of the college's continuing education program, delighted with the response to his fall and spring courses, invites him to teach an extended, summer version of the class to a group ages 50 and over. His ability to be coherent and intelligible endears him to the older students, who sometimes need things explained more clearly and in greater detail than his younger listeners.

Notably, Anthony is not a showy speaker. His wordplay is serviceable, his stage presence adequate. But he scores points with the audience by adhering to the best practices of his craft: speaking loudly enough for everyone to hear him, making eye contact with as many people as possible, delivering his words at a pace that is neither too slow nor too fast, and imbuing his speech with true, heartfelt emotion. He also asks well-timed questions that keep the audience engaged.

Most of all, Anthony ensures listeners will be able to follow his well-researched lecture easily, by using transition phrases and words that indicate a change of logic or direction is imminent. Besides relying on words such as "furthermore," "in addition," and "meanwhile" to clarify the relationship between ideas, he includes linking markers like the following, shown in boldface, to give the narrative a vigorous, conversational flow:

> Popular music **always has been influenced** by technology. For instance, how many of you remember when compact discs supplanted vinyl records and tapes? [Pauses to wait for response.] It was groundbreaking at the time. But it's happening again today, as music streaming supplants CDs.

> The great technical innovation **I would like to look at this morning** forever changed the way popular singers approached the performance of a song in public. Can you tell me what breakthrough I'm thinking of? [Pauses, waits for answers.] It's the microphone.

> The microphone **is a hugely important development** because **prior to its use** in live performance, people singing in public had to develop a way to make their voices heard in the most remote corners of major auditoriums.

> Al Jolson **is an example of** a singer who developed a style as a "belter" since **that was the only way** to be heard in a pre-

microphone era. Watch this clip of Jolson singing "Toot, Toot, Tootsie! (Goo' Bye!)" in the 1927 film *The Jazz Singer,* the revolutionary first feature-length motion picture with singing and speech in several sequences.

As you watch, note how physically extraverted Jolson is onstage, how energetically he moves his body to punctuate the song. **And observe how** on the final notes of the song, he flings his arms out, apparently to give his big finish more heft and punch. [Plays video clip.]

What was your response to that performance? [Discussion.]

Now, let's see how the availability of microphones for live performance changed things. **A wonderful early exponent** of the ability of singers to put a song across with a softer, more personal approach with the advent of microphone technology was someone you are all aware of because of the song "White Christmas." And that is Bing Crosby.

I'm going to play a video of Crosby singing "Pennies from Heaven," in 1936. **While you're watching, notice how** the microphone enables Bing to produce a gentle, intimate sound. **Before the**

microphone, you would only have found that type of singing perhaps in the privacy of someone's house. [Plays audio clip.]

What is your reaction to Bing's singing in this clip? [Discussion.]

It's often said that Bing Crosby is the most important popular singer of the first half of the 20th century. But **it has been argued** that one of the most influential   artists of the entire century was Bing's successor, Frank Sinatra.

Like Bing, Sinatra explored the properties of the microphone to perfect a conversational style. **But he did it with greater interpretative panache** than Crosby. Crosby patterned his style on an "everyman" kind of sound. You hear him and you think he sounds pretty much like an average guy who sings well.

With Sinatra, the level of the art was raised, as Sinatra uses a multiplicity of skills, notably phrasing, timing, and the shading of notes, to create a sense of singing directly to one person — the listener. **Let's listen to** Sinatra's 1960 rendition of "Fools Rush In." **As you listen,** try to pick out the nuances in Sinatra's performance that make this such a complex, convincing piece of intimate singing. [Plays audio clip.] **What did you think** of this vocal? [Discussion.]

Keeping things moving can prevent the daydreaming that many students are prone to, especially when classes are held right after lunch. That said, three hours — the typical length of many non-credit college evening classes — is a long time for people to concentrate on a talking individual, even with a break provided. Minds will invariably wander as students begin thinking about food, sleep, or the next day's activities.

RESPECT THE LIMITS OF HUMAN CONCENTRATION
Speakers at conferences, meetings, and other public events confront the same issue. It is asking a lot of attendees to require them to concentrate on a speaker for 45 minutes or longer. It may even be counterproductive: it has been argued that 10 minutes may be the limit of good human concentration.[5]

All the more reason to keep spoken-word presentations crystal-clear and concise. It's great to wrap elegantly stated arguments in facts and figures that reveal the implications of talks for the average listener. But unless the speaker constructs the narrative seamlessly to allow statements and arguments to go down easily, like a delicious beverage, much of that well-researched content could go unheard and unabsorbed.

---

[5] Scott Berkun, *Confessions of a Public Speaker* (Sebastopol, CA: O'Reilly Media, Inc., 2010), 82. Berkun quotes biologist John Medina, author of *Brain Rules* (Pear Press), as saying 10 minutes is the average amount of time most people can pay attention to a topic.

THE BOTTOM LINE: BUILD A STREAMLINED NARRATIVE

Remember: unlike consumers of movies, books, and recorded music and TV programs, live audiences generally cannot replay tracks or footage or turn back pages if they fail to catch a word, phrase, or idea the first and only time it zooms by. That's why a speaker has to build the narrative to guide the listener effortlessly, from point to point. When it is done properly, the listener never hears the craft; he or she hears only the speech.

Delivery may be the most important principle in speaking, as noted at the outset of this book, but a speech is only as effective as it is easy to comprehend. Without comprehension, delivery — and everything else in speaking — is meaningless.

For that reason, Principle No. 7 is: Make Things Easy to Follow.

25 PRACTICAL APPLICATIONS OF THE SEVEN PRINCIPLES FOR SUPER SPEAKING

The journey is never ending. There's always gonna be growth, improvement, adversity; you just gotta take it all in and do what's right, continue to grow, continue to live in the moment.
~American footballer/Pittsburgh Steeler Antonio Brown

SUMMARY: We look at 25 everyday speech challenges that can be resolved through an understanding of the seven principles for super speaking.

MAKE DELIVERY THE PRIORITY

Q. How can I develop a great delivery?

A. By speaking as often as you can and critically assessing what aspects of your style help you attract the audience's attention. Start a journal. Write down your observations after each performance. Avail yourself of as much critical feedback as you can from knowledgeable parties; avoid seeking input from friends and relatives — they may lie to spare your feelings, which does you no good in the long run.

Q. How much will my fear of speaking affect my delivery?

A. It doesn't have to be a major problem if you use the practice strategies we talked about in the section on Principle No. 4, Feel the Fear, but Keep Practicing. The important thing is to push on, no matter how terrified you may be. In addition, get as much experience speaking in front of audiences as possible to boost your confidence. Feeling secure prevents fear from hampering your ability to perform naturally — and being natural is the key to effective delivery.

Q. I have limited time to perfect my delivery. What are the basic skills I need to focus on?

A. Work at making eye contact with as many members of the audience as possible; strive to speak loudly and slowly enough to be heard and understood; speak at a pace that allows you to pronounce words clearly and the audience to follow your speech; vary your word choices; keep up your energy level; and modify the tone, volume, and expressiveness of your voice. Never apologize for onstage flubs; just do your best to recover and persevere. Look for reasons to reward yourself.

Q. The standout parts of my delivery are my hand gestures and speaking voice. How can I learn to physically move around the stage to maximize the impact of my speech?

A. Practice your speech while keeping your hands still — behind your back, or in your pockets; then try to illustrate the speech using only your voice, legs, and lower body. Move among the three corners of an imaginary triangle pointing toward the audience, sharing yourself with the crowd equally at each point. Spend more time at any point if the story line's tone demands it. For instance, at an intense moment, you may need to stand still to let your words sink in. Then go back to rehearsing the speech with hand gestures as well as your legs and lower body.

Incorporate any takeaways from the exercise into your speech to make your delivery more balanced and to improve your use of physical movement.

Q. I'm going to be making a presentation on my specialty — Italian travel — on the sidelines of a free cultural festival. Attendees will be encouraged to drop in on my talk, which will be held in a small building on the festival grounds, but nothing requires them to stay. Given that people could be coming and going as I speak, what's the best way to handle the situation, from a delivery perspective? I will be showing slides, but I don't want to rely on them.

A. Crank up your energy level and reach out. More than ever, you need to have a dialogue with viewers — literally. Talk to them: ask questions. Be personal. Remember, they are there to have a good time. Match their mood. Don't be hurt if they leave; as you say, they are not expected to stay long. Be prepared to repeat things as the audience keeps changing. If you use slides, make sure you're able to see the eyes of the spectators as you speak. Be as charismatic as possible. Keep a stack of business cards by the door.

PUT ON A SHOW

Q. I'm delivering an evening talk at a public library. The air conditioning unit is malfunctioning. Members of my audience are fanning themselves and shifting around restlessly. Should I just keep going, to get this ordeal over with? Or should I make some adjustments?

A. Adjust the speech — and the program. Given that conditions are growing more oppressive by the minute, speak for a shorter time and turn the rest of the program into a question-and-answer session; then wrap it up (the librarians likely will support your decision to end early). But stay behind to chat and to hand out business cards.

Q. In the past, one or two people at the back of the room have complained about not being able to hear me. Do I need to check the acoustics before I speak?

A. Absolutely. Visit the back of the room to evaluate how well the sound carries, from the point of view of an audience member in the last row. It's helpful to do this when someone is actually speaking. Your investigation should tell you how much louder you need to speak when you take the stage. If you have to use a microphone, and no sound check is to be done before you speak, make the trip to the back of the room when someone else is speaking to determine if every word can be heard clearly. If the sound is substandard, privately and politely ask whoever is running the public-address system to adjust it. Take these proactive steps to avoid having to ask the audience when you are onstage if they can hear you, because it takes the focus off your speech.

Q. I'm dying to be funny in a speech. Is that smart?

A. Humor is great — audiences love it. But it should be handled with care, given that everyone's sense of humor is different. So, rather than going for big laughs with isolated jokes, try to integrate your humor into the narrative. That way, if your efforts fall flat, the speech won't suffer collateral damage.

Q. What if I suddenly forget what I want to say while I am onstage?

A. Don't panic. Calmly stop speaking or moving. That will protect the show temporarily while you work this out. Picture the list of key words you made at home and initially used to learn the speech. Backtrack in your mind till the words of your speech start to come to you. Then go forward. You may wind up jumping over a piece of content, but don't worry about it. Don't let on that you have forgotten something, or apologize for it — that would only disrupt the proceedings. What's more, the audience may not even notice anything was amiss.

Q. What techniques can I use to remember my speech?

A. Key words are a reliable memory aid because you create them from your own words and feelings. Once you craft the speech in full sentences, pull out just one or two key words per paragraph that appeal to your emotions or senses. Keep discarding or trying different key words as you practice, to nail down the ones that help you remember the text best. While other memory aids exist, one size does not fit all. The best speech memory aid is the one that works for you.

Q. Why is it OK to pick key words out of full sentences but not OK to memorize a speech word for word?

A. The only time you should use the full-sentence version of a speech is to extract key words. If you try to present a speech you have memorized, word for word, you are likely to fail to click with the audience, because your focus will be on recalling all those words instead of sharing yourself with the people in the seats. You will also struggle to sound natural. By contrast, when you use key words, you can fill in around them with whatever words you like, decreasing the pressure to remember the speech.

DISPLAY PERSONALITY

Q. What's wrong with just reading a speech to an audience?

A. Lowering your eyes to read a "script" from a piece of paper, a phone, or a tablet interferes with your ability to make eye contact with the audience. When you read, your energy goes down into the paper or device instead of out to the crowd. Similarly, shackling yourself to exact words deprives you of the opportunity to speak naturally, which is crucial in revealing who you are and helping the audience to decide whether to join your exclusive club.

Q. How can I make the audience like me?

A. Smile. Use humor, but remember that your chances of not offending people will be better if you strive to be amusing rather than go for big laughs. Be friendly. Be engaging. Share yourself with the crowd physically by moving around the stage. Ask questions to get the audience engaged. Give them a reason to take an interest in your material. Be energetic. That said, there is no guarantee any of this will make them like you, but it might get them to listen to you, which is the worthier goal in the long run.

Q. Is it good to use PowerPoint — a common presentation aid — to help me get my message across?

A. It depends on the room. If turning off the lights to show slides plunges the room into darkness, you will lose eye contact with the audience — and your ability to create a dialogue with the crowd. However, if you can dim the lights so the slides are visible but you and the audience can still make eye contact, great. If you are speaking onstage under a spotlight while slides are projected above you on a screen, that is fine, too, as long as your slides are designed to complement, not distract from, your words.

FEEL THE FEAR BUT KEEP PRACTICING

Q. I'm afraid the audience will judge me harshly once I start speaking. What can I do about that?

A. Remember, when you walk out onstage, they may not be focusing on you. Often, they've got other things on their minds. They are also willing to give you a chance to engage them. So you have more time than you think to get off on a good foot.

Q. What's the best way to practice my speech?

A. After you have created a design, using full sentences, practice reading the speech into your phone recorder for flow. If it feels right, start turning your complete sentences into key words. Then try delivering the speech from key words, again recording it. Adjust the order of the key words as you see fit. When you feel comfortable, practice in front of the video camera on your computer or phone. Review the results honestly and critically. What aspects need work? Think of ways to incorporate physical movement. What kind of actions or gestures would fit where? Try to practice in a space that most closely resembles the performance area. Bounce a performance off a mentor or someone whose opinion you value. Be wary of trying out the speech on family members, since they may lie to avoid hurting your feelings. Strive to decrease the number of times you need to look at the list of key words, and try to rely more on your memory of the list, so you can interact more freely with the crowd. If it helps you remember the key words, try employing a mnemonic device, which uses mental imagery to retrieve information.

GIVE THE AUDIENCE A REASON TO CARE

Q. My audience looks bored. How can I change that?

A. Interact with them. Turn statements into questions requiring a show of hands. Look in the eyes of more people as you speak. Check your pacing — are you speaking too slowly? Pick it up, without compromising the integrity of your presentation. Are you varying the volume, the tone, and the rise and fall of your voice? Try changing those elements. Are you moving around the floor sufficiently to build interest? Are you underscoring points with hand gestures? Consider making your physical movements more purposeful and theatrical.

Q. How can I build credibility and trust with the audience?

A. Anticipate their questions before you deliver the speech, if possible. Strive to answer them in a way that establishes you have studied the facts of the matter and that you aren't just giving your opinion. If you're talking about a contentious topic, present multiple sides of the issue to provide balance.

Q. I am going to deliver a talk at a conference. How can I give the paying customers good value for their money?

A. Expand the talk by including contextual information that speaks to an enlightening trend, idea, or back story that is relevant to the audience's interests. Don't take their level of knowledge for granted. Go deeper. Just as audiences need help knowing what is worth their attention, they also need help figuring out what is worth knowing.

Q. I'm speaking at a banquet. How do I give a light, amusing speech while still keeping the audience invested?

A. By putting on a great little show. Incorporate even more show elements into your talk, and spend more time interacting with the crowd and using the stage area to connect with them. Turn up the humor. While going for profound insight here might be a stretch and even a bit out of

HOW TO BECOME A SUPER SPEAKER

place, there's nothing wrong with providing a sober reflection on how nice it is for people with a common interest — whatever that may be — to enjoy a pleasant evening together.

REVEAL WHAT'S INSIDE YOU

Q. I'm not certain I could let myself go, the way I see musicians or other entertainers do. What do I need to understand?

A. Musicians are performers who realize that audiences want to see them having a good time expressing their love of their craft. As you gain experience onstage, expressing yourself publicly will feel more natural and your inhibitions will fade.

Q. I'm afraid to deliver a speech that will draw out my emotions because I might lose control in front of everyone. Is that an unreasonable view?

A. It's your view, which is what matters. However, if you want to be an engaging performer, you have to let go of your need for control. Stage experiences are unpredictable. Say you are a guest speaker at the breakfast meeting of a local service club. You could be in the middle of your talk when someone sitting at the table in front of you accidentally knocks over a glass of water. You need to have the presence of mind to pause, let the commotion settle, and then move on — but only after you say something like: "I guess I made a big splash at that table." If you lean into your feelings, the audience will gravitate to you and you'll leave a long-lasting impression.

MAKE THINGS EASY TO FOLLOW

Q. People have told me they have trouble following my speeches. How can I fix that?

A. Since those listening to a speech don't have the luxury of being able to flip pages backward or replay a track to rehear something they may have missed, you must provide "signpost" transition phrases, or words that let the audience know that a change of logic or tone or context is coming up. For example:

> **Meanwhile**, the venerable filmmaker **wasn't going to sit idly by** while critics savaged what he considered his masterpiece. **By the end of the following week**, the director had launched an unprecedented campaign to call out the press for what he termed "mindless, irresponsible reporting."

> The ploy seemed to pay off, **for by the time the Academy Awards rolled around**, Vaughan already was being hailed as a genius for what was now being called a misunderstood cinematic triumph.

> **However,** other powerful directors **have fared less well** when they tried to start a war of words with the Fourth Estate.

Q. What's an easy way to test my speech's story line for clarity and flow?

A. In addition to using the transition-alerting words mentioned above, try to structure the speech so that when you line up the key words from start to finish, they replicate the story line. Practice delivering the speech from the key words and adjusting them as necessary until you get a clear, logical, easily flowing narrative.

Q. How do I create key words that work for me?

A. Try writing out your speech in full sentences first; then ruthlessly go through it, cutting everything except the two or three words or phrases per sentence that draw the biggest emotional response from you. Keep testing the key words and changing them until you are 100 percent convinced they would help you remember the speech even in the most pressure-filled situations.

CONCLUSION:
CLOSE IN ON YOUR GOALS!

What you get by achieving your goals is not as important as what you become by achieving your goals.
~American author, salesman, and speaker Zig Ziglar

SUMMARY: Use your improved speaking skills to complete tasks, achieve your goals, and make your dreams come true.

If you have worked your way through this book, it should be clear by now that the seven principles of super speaking are about more than simply engaging the audience or making the speaker memorable, as important as those goals are. The principles, like the eons-old practice of public speaking itself, are about honoring the audience.

When we honor the audience, something magical happens: they become more willing to honor us in return. With a path for meaningful communication established, performers and spectators become freer to experience the thrill of bonding. For just as there is no more intoxicating feeling for a performer than connecting with the crowd, there is no greater pleasure for the crowd than clicking with the performer.

With that heady sensation comes a tremendous awareness and appreciation of what is best about ourselves; and in this meeting of minds and hearts, there is also a palpable sense of what is best about being human. Such is the power of pure communication.

As you practice the principles described in this book, I hope that you do indeed gain confidence in speaking that will allow you to pursue your goals and dreams more effectively. If there are times when you doubt yourself, stay focused and keep striving; success may be just around the corner.

And if you must doubt something, as author Price Pritchett says, doubt your limits.

RESOURCES

"Apple Music Event 2001 — The First Ever iPod
Introduction." YouTube, April 3, 2006.
https://www.youtube.com/watch?v=kN0SVBCJqLs.

Berkun, Scott. *Confessions of a Public Speaker.* Sebastopol, CA:
O'Reilly Media, Inc, 2010.

Brainy Quote, https://www.brainyquote.com.

Friedwald, Will. *Jazz Singing: America's Great Voices from Bessie
Smith to Bebop and Beyond.* New York: Charles
Scribner's Sons, 1990.

Friedwald, Will. *Sinatra! The Song is You.* New York: Scribner,
1995.

Gershman, Sarah. "To Overcome Your Fear of Public
Speaking, Stop Thinking about Yourself." *Harvard
Business Review.* Sept. 17, 2019.
https://hbr.org/2019/09/to-overcome-your-fear-of-
public-speaking-stop-thinking-about-yourself

Giddins, Gary. *Bing Crosby: A Pocketful of Dreams: The Early
Years, 1903-1940.* Boston: Little, Brown and Company,
2001.

Katz, James E., ed. *Mobile Communication: Dimensions of Social
Policy.* New Brunswick, NJ: Transaction Publishers,
2011.

Morgan, Nick. "Why We Fear Public Speaking and How to Overcome It." *Forbes*, March 30, 2011. https://www.forbes.com/sites/nickmorgan/2011/03/30/why-we-fear-public-speaking-and-how-to-overcome-it/ - 3e8f5869460b

Pritchett, Price. *You²: A High-Velocity Formula for Multiplying Your Personal Effectiveness in Quantum Leaps.* Dallas, Texas: Pritchett, 1994.

Rogers, David L. *The Digital Transformation Playbook.* New York: Columbia Business School Publishing, 2016.

Schadler, Ted, and Bernoff, Josh, and Ask, Julie. *The Mobile Mind Shift: Engineer Your Business to Win in the Mobile Moment.* Cambridge, MA: Groundswell Press, 2014.

Vitelli, Romeo. "The Return of Dr. Fox." *Psychology Today*, May 5, 2014. https://www.psychologytoday.com/us/blog/media-spotlight/201405/the-return-d-fox.

If you must doubt something, doubt your limits.

~American business consultant and author
Price Pritchett

ABOUT THE AUTHOR

Michael Barris is an acclaimed transformational coach who has helped speakers of all levels learn to manage the fear of public speaking. An award-winning speaker, musician, journalist, and instructor, Mr. Barris has taken the mystery out of controlling speech anxiety for numerous executives, students, professors, and others. He emphasizes an understanding of the principles that drive the dynamic between speakers and audiences.

With a bachelor of arts in English, a bachelor of education, and a master of arts in communication, his writings include *The Social Media President: Barack Obama and the Politics of Digital Engagement* (Palgrave Macmillan), coauthored with communication scholar James E. Katz. Mr. Barris has also written scores of pieces for the *Wall Street Journal* and has been the voice of academics and business professionals in books and articles as a ghostwriter and public communicator.

His experiences as an acclaimed Rutgers University public speaking instructor and a guitarist-singer at clubs and festivals have influenced his teaching of the art of connecting with audiences.

Made in the USA
Columbia, SC
28 April 2021